MISERABLE UNSAVING

A Poetic Satire on Money Mindset for
Non-Savings Upbringings

CHARLES MWEWA

DEDICATION

.

For

all those like me, who were born and grew up, partly,
in non-savings families or countries

CONTENTS

AUTHOR'S WORD

This is a brief satire, set in poetic verse, and aimed at stimulating thought and sense. The author understands that there are those like him who grew up in contexts where money was neither planned for nor saved.

Learning how to save money either at advanced age or from the scratch if one was born in non-money-savings homes or nations, may be a challenge. But the way to prosperity passes through savings, and the author hopes that his goal will be realized.

After reading this little explicate, kindly pass it on to someone else who may need it. In this way, we all can make savings a necessary part of our lives, no matter in which context, country or situation we may be born or found.

c.m.

MISERABLE UNSAVING

Unsaving, Not Loving

O h, misery, misery, miserable
unsaving
The story of my people is almost
loving

But their habits regarding money not so
They spend everything with no flow

And then they look for chances to beg
From whence their hopes they duly peg.

1

Small Changes, Big Exchanges

They overlook small changes and more
And they are consumers to the core.

They have plans they want others to fund
And when given business, it they shunned.

They live on fertile lands, but grow no crop
Yet, every day, they spend money at a shop.

They drink alcohol from Monday to Monday
And attend church from Sunday to Sunday.

They are busy every second, and broke, too,
So, they pray for handouts, that they do.

Stash the Cash

They love you only when they see cash
And they ignore you if there's no stash;

They are sharp as a deliberate serpent
But can't account for what they spent.

They keep tide of all their inventories
If you can't, you're one of their outlawries.

They smile for as long as you can give;
Once you're drained, they quickly leave.

They look outside, often to the West
And, if nothing there, then to the East.

Lands, Not Alms

They neglect their own land, leaving it bare,
But line up in churches for alms and prayer.

They don't know God answered them already
But their own end, they have kept unsteady.

They want easy things, quick fixes, early rains
But they ate their seed, fed not their brains.

You can give them wealth, hidden in books
But they despise it, and only go for good looks.

Someone told them that they are very poor,
So, they believed it, and many are not a doer.

Government, Only as a Last Resort

They're quick to run for and to their
government
Which is also quick for donors' lineament.

They don't save for future emergencies,
But they do have numerous divergencies.

Strangely, each one has one or two cellphones
Daily they find talktime and don't take loans.

So, they make the cell companies very rich
But they are poorer, financially they twitch.

Learn and Earn

Oh, my people, they make me feel concerned,
No-one values knowledge, they've not learned.

I wrote many books for them for
empowerment;
They neither read nor kept them for
devourment.

They move in masses where there is a patron;
Anyone who can promise fringes, even a
matron.

They still see themselves as pawns of a master,
And many can only afford to excel as a pastor.

Please God, Make Money

To God be all the glory they love Christ Jesus,
But they less please Him than they please us.

This, too, gets me nervous and very troubled,
Their heavenly reward may not be doubled.

They have minds, but I am afraid they'ren't
used;
They can reinvent themselves and not be
abused,

But they must learn to understand money,
And know that there are bees before honey.

Beautiful and Fruitful

Just like to enjoy a beautiful red or pink rose,
One must learn to survive the thorny blows.

Let me tell you, my people, nothing but the
truth,
So that you may not waste your worth or
youth.

That money does not grow on trees or build
mounds,
But it's everywhere in many, any amounts.

You Can Be What You See

Money is everywhere you live, just look around
and see,
If you do so, you can be anything you want to
be.

But you must use your brain, and connect and
think,
And you will begin to have money before you
blink.

Your hands can make anything if you will;
Your legs can go in the right direction for a
thrill.

Nothing Flows Like Currency

If you can start with what doesn't need
currency,
And there are many examples, including
courtesy,

You can create opportunities and even
chances,
And begin to reap harvests and good finances.

By its nature, money may make good people
bad,
And it can bring wars and even make others
sad.

Money Doesn't Discriminate

Money can stimulate biases and discrimination
And bring enmity one nation against another
nation.

Employers can refuse to hire one for the same
And may refuse one due just to their name.

Some people are evil, they may demand sex;
Others are nepotistic and may cause you to
vex.

While others may deny you a job due to
hatred,
Or for such dubious reasons as creed's sacred.

Skillset is Realties

That is why you must hone out your own skill,
And your own destiny and future yourself drill.

You must dream of owning lands and
property,
Only by having these can you be at liberty.

Some will scheme against and you they'll boss,
All they want is for you to suffer a major loss,

And that might mean being their servants
Or slaves or any other form of disturbance.

Beg Only as Last Option

They may enjoy watching, begging for a meal
And struggling to have vegetables and veal.

Some people are filled with depravity and
greed
And they care not of whom they can't feed.

If you depend on another for a living, you're
wrong,
Because no other human can help you for
long;

They may contract a disease or may even die
And you will remain with many bills to pay.

Trust in God

You're your worst enemy if you trust others;
No-one is trustworthy, fathers or mothers.

Your own siblings, such as your own sisters,
Or brothers, may have their own family
twisters,

And they may be unwilling to help or share,
So, work hard for your own living to care.

Find something of value you can exchange;
From it, do make yourself some valuable
change.

Be Sure to Secure

Having money will give you a sense of security,
But agony only they have who rely on charity.

You must learn to work not only hard but
smart,
And that way you will surely protect your own
heart.

I am teaching you to think money to earn
And I hope that you can work wisely and
learn.

ABOUT THE AUTHOR

Award-Winning, Best-Selling Author, Charles Mwewa
(LLB; BA Law; BA Ed; LLM), is a prolific researcher, poet,
novelist, lawyer, law professor and Christian apologist and
intercessor. Mwewa has written no less than 100 books and
counting in every genre and has exhibited his works at
prestigious expos like the Ottawa International Book Expo
and is the winner of the Coppa Awards for his signature
publication, *Zambia: Struggles of My People*.
Mwewa and his family live in the Canadian Capital City of
Ottawa.

SELECTED BOOKS BY THIS AUTHOR

INDEX

www.ingramcontent.com/pod-product-compliance
Lightning Source LLC
Chambersburg PA
CBHW070722210326
41520CB00016B/4425